Public Policy, School Reform, and Special Education

A PRACTICAL APPROACH TO SPECIAL EDUCATION FOR EVERY TEACHER

The Fundamentals of Special Education
A Practical Guide for Every Teacher

The Legal Foundations of Special Education
A Practical Guide for Every Teacher

Effective Assessment for Students With Special Needs
A Practical Guide for Every Teacher

Effective Instruction for Students With Special Needs
A Practical Guide for Every Teacher

Working With Families and Community Agencies to Support Students With Special Needs
A Practical Guide for Every Teacher

Public Policy, School Reform, and Special Education
A Practical Guide for Every Teacher

Teaching Students With Sensory Disabilities
A Practical Guide for Every Teacher

Teaching Students With Medical, Physical, and Multiple Disabilities
A Practical Guide for Every Teacher

Teaching Students With Learning Disabilities
A Practical Guide for Every Teacher

Teaching Students With Communication Disorders
A Practical Guide for Every Teacher

Teaching Students With Emotional Disturbance
A Practical Guide for Every Teacher

Teaching Students With Mental Retardation
A Practical Guide for Every Teacher

Teaching Students With Gifts and Talents
A Practical Guide for Every Teacher

PUBLIC POLICY, SCHOOL REFORM, AND SPECIAL EDUCATION

A Practical Guide for Every Teacher

JIM YSSELDYKE
BOB ALGOZZINE

CORWIN PRESS
A SAGE Publications Company
Thousand Oaks, California

KH

For information:

Corwin Press
A Sage Publications Company
2455 Teller Road
Thousand Oaks, California 91320
www.corwinpress.com

Sage Publications Ltd.
1 Oliver's Yard
55 City Road
London EC1Y 1SP
United Kingdom

Sage Publications India Pvt. Ltd.
B-42, Panchsheel Enclave
Post Box 4109
New Delhi 110 017 India

Printed in the United States of America

Library of Congress Cataloging-in-Publication Data

Ysseldyke, James E.
Public policy, school reform, and special education: A practical guide
for every teacher / James E. Ysseldyke & Bob Algozzine.
     p. cm.
Includes bibliographical references and index.
ISBN 1-4129-3946-1 (cloth)
ISBN 1-4129-3899-6 (pbk.)
   1. Special education—Government policy—United States. 2. Special
education—Social aspects—United States. 3. Educational change—United States.
4. Special education teachers—Training of—United States.
I. Algozzine, Robert. II. Title.
LC3981.Y875 2006
379.1'190973—dc22

2005037822

This book is printed on acid-free paper.

06   07   08   09   10   9   8   7   6   5   4   3   2   1

Acquisitions Editor:	Kylee M. Liegl
Editorial Assistant:	Nadia Kashper
Production Editor:	Denise Santoyo
Copy Editor:	Karen E. Taylor
Typesetter:	C&M Digitals (P) Ltd.
Indexer:	Kathy Paparchontis
Cover Designer:	Michael Dubowe

6/12/06 ✓ 16 of 13

Contents

About
A Practical Approach to Special Education for Every Teacher

Special education means specially designed instruction for students with unique learning needs. Students receive special education for many reasons. Students with disabilities such as mental retardation, hearing impairments (including deafness), speech or language impairments, visual impairments (including blindness), emotional disturbance, orthopedic impairments, autism, traumatic brain injury, other health impairments, or specific learning disabilities are entitled to special education services. Students who are gifted and talented also receive special education. Special education services are delivered in many settings, including regular classes, resource rooms, and separate classes. The 13 books of this collection will help you teach students with disabilities and those with gifts and talents. Each book focuses on a specific area of special education and can be used individually or in conjunction with all or some of the other books. Six of the books provide the background and content knowledge you need in order to work effectively with all students with unique learning needs:

Book 1: The Fundamentals of Special Education

Book 2: The Legal Foundations of Special Education

Book 3: Effective Assessment for Students With Special Needs

Book 4: Effective Instruction for Students With Special Needs

Book 5: Working With Families and Community Agencies to Support Students With Special Needs

Book 6: Public Policy, School Reform, and Special Education

Seven of the books focus on teaching specific groups of students who receive special education:

Book 7:   Teaching Students With Sensory Disabilities

Book 8:   Teaching Students With Medical, Physical, and Multiple Disabilities

Book 9:   Teaching Students With Learning Disabilities

Book 10: Teaching Students With Communication Disorders

Book 11: Teaching Students With Emotional Disturbance

Book 12: Teaching Students With Mental Retardation

Book 13: Teaching Students With Gifts and Talents

All of the books in *A Practical Approach to Special Education for Every Teacher* will help you to make a difference in the lives of all students, especially those with unique learning needs.

ACKNOWLEDGMENTS

The approach we take in *A Practical Approach to Special Education for Every Teacher* is an effort to change how professionals learn about special education. The 13 separate books are a result of prodding from our students and from professionals in the field to provide a set of materials that "cut to the chase" in teaching them about students with disabilities and about building the capacity of systems to meet those students' needs. Teachers told us that in their classes they always confront students with special learning needs and students their school district has assigned a label to (e.g., students with learning disabilities). Our students and the professionals we worked with wanted a very practical set of texts that gave them the necessary **information** *about* **the students** (e.g., federal definitions, student characteristics) and specific **information on** *what to do about* **the students** (assessment and teaching strategies, approaches that work). They also wanted the opportunity to purchase parts of textbooks, rather than entire texts, to learn what they needed.

The production of this collection would not have been possible without the support and assistance of many colleagues. Professionals associated with Corwin Press—Faye Zucker, Kylee Liegl, Robb Clouse—helped us work through the idea of introducing special education differently, and their support in helping us do it is deeply appreciated.

Faye Ysseldyke and Kate Algozzine, our children, and our grandchildren also deserve recognition. They have made the problems associated with the project very easy to diminish, deal with, or dismiss. Every day in every way, they enrich our lives and make us better. We are grateful for them.

About the Authors

Jim Ysseldyke, PhD, is Birkmaier Professor in the Department of Educational Psychology, director of the School Psychology Program, and director of the Center for Reading Research at the University of Minnesota. Widely requested as a staff developer and conference speaker, he brings more than 30 years of research and teaching experience to educational professionals around the globe.

As the former director of the federally funded National Center on Educational Outcomes, Ysseldyke conducted research and provided technical support that helped to boost the academic performance of students with disabilities and improve school assessment techniques nationally. Today he continues to work to improve the education of students with disabilities.

The author of more than 300 publications on special education and school psychology, Ysseldyke is best known for his textbooks on assessment, effective instruction, issues in special education, and other cutting-edge areas of education and school psychology. With *A Practical Approach to Special Education for Every Teacher,* he seeks to equip educators with practical knowledge and methods that will help them to better engage students in exploring—and meeting—all their potentials.

Bob Algozzine, PhD, is professor in the Department of Educational Leadership at the University of North Carolina at Charlotte and project codirector of the U.S. Department of Education–supported Behavior and Reading Improvement Center. With 25 years of research experience and extensive first-hand knowledge of teaching students classified as seriously emotionally disturbed (and other equally useless terms), Algozzine is a uniquely qualified staff developer, conference speaker, and teacher of behavior management and effective teaching courses.

As an active partner and collaborator with professionals in the Charlotte-Mecklenburg schools in North Carolina and as an editor of several journals focused on special education, Algozzine keeps his finger on the pulse of current special education practice. He has written more than 250 manuscripts on special education topics, authoring many popular books and textbooks on how to manage emotional and social behavior problems. Through *A Practical Approach to Special Education for Every Teacher*, Algozzine hopes to continue to help improve the lives of students with special needs—and the professionals who teach them.

Self-Assessment 1

Before you begin this book, check your knowledge of the content being covered. Choose the best answer for each of the following questions:

1. Which of the following is NOT a driving force behind change in special education?

   a. Social factors

   b. Political factors

   c. Personal factors

   d. Economic factors

2. In recent years, while the number of students classified as having mental retardation has decreased, those classified as having learning disabilities has _____.

   a. Decreased

   b. Increased

   c. Stayed the same

   d. Doubled

3. Head Start is an example of a(n) _____, a way to help disadvantaged children acquire learning readiness skills.

   a. Early intervention

   b. Special education

   c. Site-based management

   d. Advocacy group

4. Which of the following currently provides the most funding for public education?

   a. Local governments

   b. State governments

   c. Federal government

   d. Private foundations

5. No Child Left Behind mandates which of the following?

   a. Content standards

   b. Lifelong learning

   c. Spending

   d. Accountability

6. Which of the following was NOT addressed in "Goals 2000," an education plan created in 1994 by George H. W. Bush and endorsed by Bill Clinton?

   a. Mathematics and science

   b. Parental participation

   c. Students with special needs

   d. Teacher education and professional development

7. Site-based management includes which of the following restructuring changes?

   a. Decision making at the central office

   b. Changing staff roles

   c. Emphasis on basic skills

   d. Budget cuts

8. Which of the following is NOT an example of a standard?

   a. Criteria for achievement level

   b. Desirable characteristic for action

c. Necessary core of knowledge

d. Important piece of information

9. A system which abolishes the distinctions between general education and special education is known as a _____.

   a. Unified system

   b. Partial system

   c. Conglomerate system

   d. Modern system

10. For a given student, the "least restrictive environment" could be a _____.

    a. General education classroom

    b. Special education classroom

    c. General education classroom with support

    d. All of the above

REFLECTION

- Identify three alternative explanations for why special education services may be different in Detroit, Miami, and Missoula, Montana.
- What are three major things that happened to public education as a result of passage of the No Child Left Behind Act?
- In this chapter, we argue that education in the U.S. is driven by two goals: excellence and equity. Describe these twin goals, and indicate briefly how schools might possibly work to meet both.

Introduction to
Public Policy, School Reform, and Special Education

Lenny is a brilliant student of mathematics and **Sarah** is the best chess player in her hometown, perhaps in the country. **C.J.** and **Bobby** are students with physical disabilities, one with and one without special learning needs. **Terry** is known as a "living legend" at Magnolia Middle School and is a student who repeatedly engages in disturbing behaviors. **Xong** migrated from Cambodia and is more than two years below her fifth-grade classmates.

Among these students, who should receive special education services?

What is education in the U.S. all about, and what are its goals? Should the goals be the same for Lenny, Terry, C.J., and Xong? Should the curriculum be easier for some of these students than others? Special education services are costly. Are educators' time and society's money better spent remediating Xong's language difficulties and experience deficits, or enhancing Lenny's outstanding math skills? Will society be better if Sarah builds her math skills to specialize in satellite telecommunications, or if Terry stays out of jail?

The delivery of educational services to students who are exceptional is a dynamic enterprise. Between the time we write this module and the time you read it, major changes will have taken place. Changes in society, legislation, general education, special education, related services professions, and community agencies bring about change in delivery of educational services to all students, including those who are exceptional. The educational professions are driven by social, political, and economic factors. When there are major changes in availability of resources, in attitudes of the public toward education or toward people with disabilities, or in the federal government, there are changes in special education.

In this module, we consider broad social trends, national school reform, and public policy. We look at the current scene in education with a focus on the delivery of educational services to students who are exceptional. On occasion, we take a glimpse at the origins of current activities, and we discuss questions that educators will face in the future.

1

What Factors Drive Special Education?

On the broadest scale, special education is driven by social, political, and economic factors. These three factors do not operate independently; they interact. For example, the Head Start program, created in 1965, is a program of intervention for disadvantaged preschool children. Is Head Start a social, political, or economic innovation? Clearly the program had social origins and benefits: Providing educational opportunities for disadvantaged preschoolers improves their chances for success in later schooling and reduces the likelihood of their needing other special services. Head Start also has political origins and benefits: Members of Congress and other political organizations fought to establish the program and continue to support it. In addition, Head Start is influenced by economic factors: The costs of prevention have reduced later special-service costs, and the program has added "producers" to society.

As you read the following sections about social, political, and economic factors, bear this in mind: There are no clear distinctions among the factors that influence special education. They work together to affect the ways in which special education is practiced.

SOCIAL VALUES

Many of society's resources are limited. People hold social values, opinions, and beliefs that influence how those limited resources are distributed. These social values affect who receives special education services; who pays for them; which services are provided; and where, when, and how they are delivered. Social values are not absolute. Two people may hold different values or hold the same values to varying degrees. For some, education is a critical social value; for others, it is less important than a new civic center, good roads, or national defense. People voice their social values by voting in local, state, and national elections for candidates who believe as they do, and by forming or joining advocacy groups.

Social values are always changing. The general social climate—national and global—has a strong impact on educational policy. Social attitudes toward education in general and toward aspects of special education shifted radically, for example, after the Soviet Union launched the Sputnik satellite in 1957. Fear that the United States was falling behind the Soviet Union led to new programs to educate students with disabilities, disadvantaged students, and gifted students.

Changes in Classification

In recent years, a major change occurred in classification practices: The number of students classified as having mental retardation has decreased, while the number classified as having learning disabilities has dramatically increased. This change did not happen because of a sudden "cure" for mental retardation or because of an epidemic that resulted in learning disabilities. Rather, the overrepresentation of students of color in the mental retardation category led to legal challenges to the classification system. Many people also became concerned about the stigma attached to retardation. Eventually, the definition of mental retardation was refined and awareness raised, and fewer students were assigned to that category. Meanwhile, learning disabilities came to the fore as a designation with greater social acceptability. Because society could provide services for students with learning disabilities, use of that category increased.

Early Intervention

The influence of social factors on special education is probably no more apparent than it is in the education of very young children (see Ysseldyke, Algozzine, & Thurlow, 2000). Early intervention is the fastest growing area in special education. During the first part of the twentieth century, the education of very young children with special needs was a concern of a small, dedicated group of educators. Initially, private moneys financed early childhood education, and preschool programs for children with disabilities were operated largely by independent agencies (such as the United Cerebral Palsy Association) or parent organizations. Designed to provide relief for families, these programs were the first to provide educational services of direct benefit to young children. Interest in early childhood education revived during the 1960s, partly because Americans had entered a fierce scientific rivalry with the Soviet Union and partly because, as the post–World War II economy slackened, large numbers of women entered the workforce and needed child care for infants, toddlers, and preschoolers.

Shifting Responsibilities

Increasing numbers of students were not meeting the academic and behavioral standards of public schools. The Head Start program was a response to this shortcoming, a way to help disadvantaged children adapt to the educational program by giving them learning readiness skills. During the 1990s, early intervention programs had to respond to complex social issues. More and more children were being exposed prenatally to drugs such as cocaine. Each year, more babies were born with fetal alcohol syndrome. Many children had to attend to their own needs, and increasing numbers were getting their basic nutrition from schools and service agencies. Today, society seems to have relegated to schools the important responsibilities of child care and the fostering of child development—responsibilities that previously lay with families. Moreover, early intervention and elementary school programs are often expected to counteract the social effects of poverty, unemployment, racism, war, and drug abuse.

POLITICAL FACTORS

A variety of political factors, closely related to social and economic factors, have significant effects on public policy regarding the education of students with disabilities. First, the general political climate influences public policy in special education. In a liberal or progressive political climate, special education services tend to become more available; the resources for delivering services are greater. In a conservative political climate, services become limited. During the 1960s, a liberal period, many federal programs were initiated for students with disabilities and disadvantaged students. In the late 1970s and 1980s, a conservative period, fiscal restraint was evident. Major questions were raised about the benefits of special education services, funding for programs was cut, and proposals to abolish the U.S. Department of Education were made. Now, with the Elementary and Secondary Education Act, reauthorized in 2001 as the No Child Left Behind Act (Public Law 107-110), there is a push for evidence-based interventions, massive programs to support literacy instruction in the early grades (Reading First), and accountability.

Second, the political action of parents and advocacy groups shapes special education policy. Class-action lawsuits have played a major role in the last several decades. The case of *Larry P. v. Riles* (1972, 1974), for example, forced the state of California to stop using intelligence tests to place African-American students in classes for students with mental retardation. In 1993, the parents of such students again sued the California Department of Education, this time to allow their children to be given intelligence tests. It was argued that exclusion of the students from intellectual assessment might keep the students from being declared eligible for the benefits of services for students with learning disabilities. As these cases illustrate, the ramifications of legal action can be complex. Overall, however, families and advocacy groups have used the court system to win educational rights for students with disabilities, as well as protection from abusive treatment and involuntary institutionalization.

Advocacy Groups

Advocacy groups directly influence policymakers and legislators. Groups interested in special education range from broad-based organizations, such as the Council for Exceptional Children and the American Federation of Teachers, to groups concerned with particular disabilities, such as the Learning Disabilities Association of America (see Resources section). The larger and more powerful groups wield political influence through their statements and publications. When the American Federation of Teachers issues guidelines for placement of students who are exceptional, educators throughout the U.S. take notice. Many advocacy groups also employ lobbyists— experts who know how to disseminate information, sway public opinion, and pressure important legislators. Advocacy groups often band together to address issues. A group called Citizens Concerned About Disability, comprised of representatives of major professional associations and advocacy groups (usually each group is represented by a person called a government liaison), meets regularly in Washington, DC, to have a voice in legislation and federal educational and mental-health policy issues. The major educational laws of the past two decades—the laws that define special education as it exists today—are very much a result of such political influence. So are the ongoing changes in categorization, such as the relatively recent establishment of autism and traumatic brain injury as separate federal disability categories.

Government Agencies

Certain government agencies protect or further the rights of individuals who are exceptional. For example, both the U.S. Office of Civil Rights and the Bureau of Indian Affairs have

Window on Practice:
Case Study in Advocacy: Passage of Goals 2000

Goals 2000 is a federal education act that was signed in March 1994. (The act is discussed in more detail in the Goals 2000 section of this module.) It is a good example of the power of advocacy groups. The original draft of the act listed six national goals, but the final law includes eight. Where did the extra two goals come from?

During debate on the bill, teacher groups argued that if they were to provide the up-to-date instruction implied by the act, they would need greater opportunities for professional development and training. Thus a goal relating to teacher education and professional development was added to the law.

Teachers and families argued that students could not achieve the national goals without considerable family involvement and strong linkages between homes and schools. For this reason, a goal concerning family participation was added.

Other differences between the original and final drafts include:

The original draft had no specific language to indicate that the law applied to all American children, including those with disabilities. But parents of students with disabilities argued that the high educational standards specified in the act should apply to their children as well as others. In the end, such language was added.

The original bill mandated that states establish opportunity-to-learn standards (described later in this module). This provision reflected the belief that if we hold students responsible for achieving high standards, we should also hold schools and school personnel responsible for delivering the related instruction. But teacher unions and others actively opposed this requirement. As a result, in the law's final language, the opportunity-to-learn standards became voluntary rather than mandatory for the states.

> The law's original version mentioned only certain academic subjects. The final version named a number of other subjects because groups of teachers representing the omitted subject areas successfully lobbied for their inclusion.
>
> These changes were neither unusual nor unexpected. Goals 2000 is merely one instance of the major role played by advocacy groups in formulating public policy on education.

influenced the provision of services for those with disabilities. Thus a federal or state bureaucracy can itself become an important political factor.

ECONOMIC FACTORS

Who pays for special education? Public education dollars come from federal, state, and local governments. For many years, local governments provided the largest share. In the 1978–79 school year, however, the state share of funding rose above the local share (Stern, 1988), and the state contribution has remained higher ever since.

When in 1975 it enacted the Education for All Handicapped Children Act, now the Individuals With Disabilities Education Act (1990), Congress assigned the responsibility for providing a free, appropriate public education to all children with disabilities to state and local governments. However, state educational agencies and local school districts get federal financial assistance in implementing the nation's special education mandates. Along with this financial help, the federal government provides supervision, policy support, and technical assistance.

OSEP Programs

The Office of Special Education Programs (OSEP) in the U.S. Department of Education administers two funding programs:

the IDEA Part B State Grant Program and the Chapter 1 Program for Children With Disabilities. Under the IDEA Part B State Grant Program, funds are distributed to states according to the total numbers of students with disabilities reported as receiving special education and related services. State educational agencies conduct an annual child count on December 1 of the previous fiscal year and submit these counts to OSEP.

Funds appropriated by OSEP during federal fiscal year (FFY) 2004 amounted to approximately $14.2 billion, with a request for approximately $15.4 billion in FFY 2005. At least 75 percent of the funds that a state receives under the IDEA Part B State Grant Program must be distributed to local educational agencies and intermediate educational units to assist in the education of students with disabilities. Local education agencies must certify to the state that they are not using these funds to replace local funding, but to pay for excess costs of educating students with disabilities.

Federal Review of State Plans

The U.S. Department of Education attaches "strings" to such allocations. States must submit program goals, objectives, strategies, and priorities annually to the secretary of education for review and approval. State plans are reviewed to spot deficiencies in service delivery. To receive its funding, the state must provide the assurance that it will implement corrected procedures during the forthcoming year and that all deficiencies in the plan will be corrected before the next grant cycle.

On-site monitoring reviews are another important component of the federal program-review process. Each state that receives financial assistance is visited about every three years by a monitoring team from the U.S. Department of Education. The team visits the state education agency and representative local education agencies. In addition to reviewing a state's written policies and procedures, members of the monitoring team solicit information from families, the general public, advocates, and representatives of professional groups. They hold public meetings and solicit written testimony on the quality of service provided by the state.

Competition for Funding

The federal monitoring process produces a degree of uncertainty in educational funding; federal money is not automatic. Another source of uncertainty is that education is only one among many social services that the government provides. General and special education must compete for dollars with highways, sanitation, and other services. To the extent that members of society value special education more than other services, special education is financed more heavily. Special education also competes with general education for financial resources. From all the funds provided for education, moneys must be allocated between general and special education. When a state increases the moneys allocated to special education, moneys allocated to general education typically diminish.

Research Priorities

Government spending patterns influence public policy on the education of students who are exceptional, although those spending patterns also *reflect* public policy. If you want to know where the most research activity in special education will take place over the next five years, look at the research priorities established by the U.S. Department of Education. During the 1950s and 1960s, the federal government made mental retardation a priority, and centers for research on mental retardation were established across the country. As funding priorities changed, new centers were established, and old ones changed their names and expanded their missions. During the middle and late 1970s, institutes were funded to conduct research on learning disabilities and on early intervention. The 1980s saw less federal support for research on learning disabilities. Instead, support shifted to research on students with severe disabilities and transition services for older students with disabilities. In the 1990s, emphasis was on early childhood education. Currently, the focus has shifted to evidence-based treatments and accountability. Decisions to shift research efforts often are motivated by economics: Researchers go where the money is.

Competition Among Categorical Programs

The overall pool of money available to provide special education services must be divided among all exceptional students. This necessity creates competition for resources among the various categorical programs. If a fixed amount of money is available to educate students with disabilities, and if school personnel decide to spend a greater proportion of that money on educating students who are deaf, then less money is available for educating students with other exceptionalities.

Allocation Methods

Technical methods of funding allocation also influence special education services. State legislatures decide how much state money will be allocated to the education of students who are exceptional, and they decide how the state moneys and the funds received from the federal government will be distributed to local education agencies. There are various criteria for these decisions.

Some states allocate funds according to the number of "teacher units." That is, for each school district, the state determines a reasonable number of special education personnel on the basis of community demographics; then the state provides a certain percentage of those people's salaries. This method discourages schools from identifying large numbers of students with disabilities. More students mean larger special education classes, but not more money; hence, schools often develop informal policies that inhibit teachers from identifying students with special education needs.

Other states use a "pupil unit" method of allocation. This method is based on the assumption that it costs more to educate students with disabilities than students who are not disabled. The largest extra cost is for special education personnel; other costs include specially designed transportation, food services, equipment, and health and rehabilitation services. State departments of education typically pay school districts a subsidy for each student. In the per-pupil method of allocation, the state makes up for the extra cost of educating students with disabilities by increasing the subsidy for each of these students. For example, if the state calculates that students with disabilities are 2.4 times more expensive to educate than those without disabilities, the state multiplies its subsidy by 2.4 for every student in the district who is classified as disabled. Average per-pupil costs vary from state to state, as do extra costs. The pupil-unit method seems fairer than the teacher-unit method. However, it encourages "bounty hunting" by school district administrators who may manipulate the number of students classified as disabled in order to increase the district's subsidy.

Some states, recognizing that certain disabilities require greater educational expenses than others, use a specific multiplier for each disability category. The state education department might decide that educating students who are blind costs twice as much as educating those with learning disabilities, and adjust the subsidies accordingly. Even this system can be manipulated; schools may label their students according to expected financial return rather than according to needs.

In times of financial prosperity, these economic considerations may fade. If money is not an issue, schools seldom attempt to limit services to students who are exceptional or to restrict the number of students declared eligible. For most public school districts, however, times have not been prosperous. Furthermore, the enrollment of greater numbers of students with severe disabilities in public education programs has increased the financial burden on schools. Buildings and equipment must be modified, and new equipment and facilities purchased. Because schools must provide education and *related* services, they end up paying for communication boards, hearing aids, and other devices. As the financial burden increases, educators become concerned about the number of students receiving special education and about who will pay the costs. There is a tenuous balance between society's desire to provide special education services and its ability to pay for them.

2

What Should Every Teacher Know About School Reform?

A s the previous sections indicate, social, political, and economic factors continually shift, and their total effect on education changes over time. Since the early 1980s, various factors have combined to spur a strong movement toward school reform. Considerable reform activity is under way. Some reforms are prompted by economic concerns, especially about the limited funding now available. Many reform efforts stem from social and political concerns, particularly the concern that quality of schooling is not as good as society would like. Various reports have identified areas in which America's schools are lacking, or in which American youth fall behind youth from other countries. The following sections describe efforts to establish national education goals, national standards, and opportunity-to-learn standards. We also describe efforts to restructure schools and discuss the implications of all these efforts.

NATIONAL EDUCATION GOALS

In 1983, the National Commission on Excellence in Education produced a report entitled *A Nation at Risk: The Imperative for*

Educational Reform. The report was critical of American schooling and called for a commitment to excellence—higher standards, more courses, more homework, more time in school, more time spent on academics, and more local and state responsibility for education. In 1984, President Reagan stated four national education goals to be reached by the year 1990:

Raise the high school graduation rate to more than 90 percent.

Raise scores on college admission tests above the 1985 average.

Make teachers' salaries competitive with entry-level business and engineering graduates' salaries.

Stiffen high school graduation requirements.

By 1990, the high school graduation rate was about 60–75 percent. (A range is reported because there is virtually no agreement on how to define and count dropouts.) Scores on college admission tests had gone up slightly, while teachers' salaries had not become competitive with entry-level business and engineering graduates' salaries. Most states were stiffening graduation requirements, such as having students pass a test to graduate. Although admirable, the goals ignored the growing number of students who needed special education services.

In 1989, the National Governors' Association published a report entitled *Time for Results.* The report called attention to the need to improve school organization and policy as well as the quality of teachers; it recognized the needs of children at risk, especially those who were very young; and it addressed the need for early intervention.

The year 2000 passed without a formal assessment of the extent to which the national education goals had been achieved. The focus shifted. Assessment and accountability became the topics of the day, and the national agenda shifted to early literacy. The Reading Excellence Act (1998) agenda of President Clinton was modified and became the Reading First initiative of the Bush administration. Focus was on getting all students to read by the end of third grade.

REI and Inclusion

When educators were thinking deeply about reform in general education, the **regular education initiative (REI)** was proposed. Despite its name, it was a call from special education for reform in the way services were provided to students with disabilities. REI called for responsibility shared by general educators and special educators for students considered disabled, with the goal of breaking down barriers between the two educational systems and integrating students with disabilities more fully into the general education classroom. Debate about the initiative was heated among most special educators and parents. Some special educators worried about the need for their services if general educators assumed responsibility for students with disabilities. Other special educators wondered whether they had the consultation skills required for the shared responsibility proposed by those who backed the initiative. Parents expressed concerns about due process rights and about whether their children would be educated appropriately. Personnel in general education knew relatively little about the initiative until years after debate about it had commenced.

The term **inclusion** or **full inclusion** has replaced REI as the focus of debate. Although inclusion means different things to different people, in general, it means including students with special needs in general education programs as much as possible. Despite the change in terminology, the issue of responsibility continues to be critical. General educators wonder whether they should assume responsibility for educating students with disabilities, especially if little teacher training is provided.

Goals 2000

As the debates over REI and inclusion erupted, the reform movement in general education continued. In 1989, President George H. W. Bush convened a meeting of the governors from the 50 states in Charlottesville, VA at an education summit. This summit resulted in a list of national education goals. The six goals were fleshed out with a set of national educational objectives and were specified in a press release from the White House (1990). The national goals were then specified in a proposal to Congress called America 2000. These national education goals were supported by then-governor of Arkansas, Bill Clinton.

When he became president, Clinton incorporated the six national goals into federal legislation as part of Goals 2000: The Educate America Act (1994). Two goals were added as the legislation passed through Congress. Goals 2000 was signed by President Clinton on March 30, 1994. The eight national goals are listed in *Table 2.1*. They focus on readiness for school, school completion, student achievement and citizenship, teacher education and development, mathematics and science, adult literacy and lifelong learning, the school environment (safe, disciplined, and drug-free schools), and family participation in children's schooling. Goals 2000 was a significant step in education reform and public policy. Its eight goals have been incorporated into subsequent legislation, so the act is rarely referred to by name any more. Still, the goals remain a vital part of public policy, and it is important that educators understand both what these goals proposed and their impact on policy and reform.

School Readiness

The focus of the first education goal was readiness for school. Three educational objectives were associated with this goal:

All children will have access to high quality and developmentally appropriate preschool programs that help prepare children for school.

Every parent in the United States will be a child's first teacher and devote time each day to helping his or her preschool child learn; and parents will have access to the training and support they need.

Children will receive the nutrition, physical activity experiences, and health care needed to arrive at school with healthy

Table 2.1 National Education Goals

Goal 1: School Readiness	By the year 2000, all children will start school ready to learn.
Goal 2: School Completion	By the year 2000, the high school graduation rate will increase to at least 90 percent.
Goal 3: Student Achievement and Citizenship	By the year 2000, all students will leave grades 4, 8, and 12 having demonstrated competency over challenging subject matter including English, mathematics, science, foreign languages, civics and government, economics, arts, history, and geography, and every school will ensure that all students learn to use their minds well, so they may be prepared for responsible citizenship, further learning, and productive employment in our nation's modern economy.
Goal 4: Teacher Education and Professional Development	By the year 2000, the nation's teaching force will have access to programs for the continued improvement of their professional skills and the opportunity to acquire the knowledge and skills needed to instruct and prepare all students for the next century.
Goal 5: Mathematics and Science	By the year 2000, United States students will be first in the world in mathematics and science achievement.

(Continued)

Table 2.1 (Continued)

Goal 6: Adult Literacy and Lifelong Learning	By the year 2000, every adult will be literate and will possess the knowledge and skills necessary to compete in a global economy and exercise the rights and responsibilities of citizenship.
Goal 7: Safe, Disciplined, and Alcohol- and Drug-Free Schools	By the year 2000, every school in the United States will be free of drugs, violence, and the unauthorized presence of firearms and alcohol and will offer a disciplined environment conducive to learning.
Goal 8: Parental Participation	By the year 2000, every school will promote partnerships that will increase parental involvement and participation in promoting the social, emotional, and academic growth of children.

Source: Goals 2000: The Educate America Act (1994).

minds and bodies, and the number of low-birthweight babies will be significantly reduced through enhanced prenatal health systems.

School Completion

The completion of high school was the focus of the second national education goal and its two objectives:

The nation will dramatically reduce its dropout rate, and 75 percent of the students who do drop out will successfully complete a high school degree or its equivalent.

The gap in high school graduation rates between American students from minority backgrounds and their nonminority counterparts will be eliminated.

This goal sounds like one of the national goals voiced by President Reagan in 1984, to be reached by 1990 ("to raise the high school graduation rate to more than 90 percent"). Like Reagan's goal, it suggests nonrecognition of students with disabilities.

Student Achievement and Citizenship

The broad notions of achievement and citizenship come together in the third educational goal, which specified competence in English, math, science, foreign languages, civics and government, economics, arts, history, and geography. It also specified preparation for responsible citizenship. These six objectives were associated with it:

The academic performance of all students at the elementary and secondary level will increase significantly in every quartile, and the distribution of minority students in each quartile will more closely reflect the student population as a whole.

The percentage of students who demonstrate the ability to reason, solve problems, apply knowledge, and write and communicate effectively will increase substantially.

All students will be involved in activities that promote and demonstrate citizenship, good health, community service, and personal responsibility.

All students will have access to physical education and health education to ensure they are healthy and fit.

The percentage of students who are competent in more than one language will substantially increase.

All students will be knowledgeable about the diverse cultural heritage of this nation and about the world community.

This goal focused on competency in various content areas and on the even broader goals of learning to use the mind to foster responsible citizenship, advanced learning, and productive employment. It reflects the move toward national and state-by-state assessments of educational indicators, which in turn has created additional questions for professionals responsible for students with disabilities. Educators debate the extent to which students with disabilities can be included in state and national testing; they argue about whether students with disabilities can attain the goals; and they debate the absence of "functional skills" from the objectives.

Teacher Education and Professional Development

Goal four was one of the two goals added during congressional debate. It specified that teachers should have access to training programs designed to improve their professional skills. It also indicated that the purpose of this professional training would be to enable students to reach the other goals and be prepared for the next century. The objectives for this goal follow:

All teachers will have access to preservice teacher education and continuing professional development activities that provide them with knowledge and skills to teach an increasingly diverse student population with a variety of educational, social, and health needs.

All teachers will have continuing opportunities to acquire additional knowledge and skills to teach challenging subject matter and to use emerging new methods, forms of assessment, and technologies.

States and school districts will create integrated strategies to attract, recruit, prepare, retrain, and support the continued professional development of teachers, administrators, and other educators, so that there is a highly talented work force of professional educators to teach challenging subject matter.

Partnerships will be established, whenever possible, among local educational agencies, institutions of higher education, parents, and among local labor, business, and professional associations to provide and support programs for the professional development of educators.

Mathematics and Science

The fifth goal called for U.S. students to be first in the world in math and science. These objectives were associated with the goal:

Mathematics and science education, including the metric system, will be strengthened throughout the system, especially in the early grades.

The number of teachers with a substantive background in mathematics and science, including the metric system, will increase by 50 percent.

The number of U.S. undergraduate and graduate students, especially women and minorities, who complete degrees in mathematics, science, and engineering will increase.

This goal targets two specific content areas for emphasis because of their significance in international business competition.

Adult Literacy and Lifelong Learning

The sixth goal was focused beyond the school setting to postschool outcomes. Here are its objectives:

Every major American business will be involved in strengthening the connection between education and work.

All workers will have the opportunity to acquire the knowledge and skills, from basic to highly technical, needed to adapt to emerging new technologies, work methods, and markets through public and private educational, vocational, technical, workplace, or other programs.

The number of quality programs, including those at libraries, that are designed to serve more effectively the needs of the growing number of part-time and mid-career students will increase substantially.

The proportion of those qualified students, especially minorities, who enter college, who complete at least two years, and who complete their degree programs will increase substantially.

The proportion of college graduates who demonstrate an advanced ability to think critically, communicate effectively, and solve problems will increase substantially.

Schools, in implementing comprehensive family involvement programs, will offer more adult literacy, parent training, and lifelong learning opportunities to improve the ties between home and school and to enhance parents' work and home lives.

This goal might be interpreted broadly as successful transition from school to work for students with disabilities. Yet the White House press release (1990) only discussed jobs that required more than a high school education, coordination of policies and programs to promote literacy, and greater access to college education for those who are qualified.

Safe, Disciplined, and Alcohol- and Drug-Free Schools

The seventh goal addressed the condition of the school environment. These objectives were associated with it:

Every school will implement a firm and fair policy on the use, possession, and distribution of drugs and alcohol.

Parents, businesses, and governmental and community organizations will work together to ensure the rights of students to study in a safe and secure environment that is free of drugs and crime, and ensure that schools provide a healthy environment and are a safe haven for all children.

Every local educational agency will develop and implement a policy to ensure that all schools are free of violence and the unauthorized presence of weapons.

Every local education agency will develop a sequential, comprehensive K–12 drug and alcohol prevention program.

Drug and alcohol curriculum will be taught as an integral part of sequential, comprehensive health education.

Community-based teams will be organized to provide students and teachers with needed support.

Every school will work to eliminate sexual harassment.

This broad goal is appropriate for all students.

Parental Participation

The eighth goal also resulted from congressional debate about Goals 2000. It was argued that holding students responsible for achieving high standards required involving families in their educational programs; therefore, the goal called for partnerships between parents and school personnel to enhance the social, emotional, and academic growth of children. The objectives for this goal follow:

Every state will develop policies to assist local schools and local educational agencies to establish programs for increasing partnerships that respond to the varying needs of families, including families of children who are disadvantaged or bilingual, or families of children with disabilities.

Every school will actively engage families in partnerships that support the academic work of children at home and shared educational decision-making at school.

Families will help to ensure that schools are adequately supported and will hold schools and teachers to high standards of accountability.

HOW THE GOALS APPLY TO STUDENTS WITH SPECIAL NEEDS

In response to these eight national education goals, special educators considered how these goals applied to students with special needs. The goals were primarily academic; they said little or nothing about social skills, life skills, or functional skills. The ways the goals were interpreted suggest that students with disabilities are neither ready to learn, nor capable of achieving world-class standards, and are likely to drop out of school. Members of the disability community long have voiced concerns about what will happen as schools focus intensely on the attainment of national goals. Will students be excluded when their developmental circumstances make it difficult for them to achieve the national goals? Will they be counted among the students who are ready to learn, who drop out, or who have world-class knowledge of math and science? If students with disabilities are not counted now, when will they count?

THE GOALS TODAY

The year 2000 has passed. What happened to Goals 2000 and its objectives? Goals 2000 is now embodied in two pieces of legislation: the amendments to the Individuals With Disabilities Education Act (2004) and the No Child Left Behind Act (2001). These two laws specify that states must have educational standards and that they must report annually on the progress of all students toward meeting those standards. Responsibility for meeting Goals 2000 has largely passed to states.

NATIONAL STANDARDS

National task forces, panels, and committees are encouraging the development of world-class standards for student performance, especially in basic skill areas. For example, Goals 2000 specified that Congress appoint a National Educational Standards and Improvement Council (NESIC). This group was responsible for certifying voluntary state-proposed standards for instruction. If a state required that students meet specific graduation criteria or master specific mathematics content, for example, NESIC decided if the standards were appropriate. Although NESIC is no longer in effect, similar groups and policies are constantly being formed to ensure that new educational standards are met.

Standards are statements of criteria against which comparisons can be made. The term **standards** has several educational meanings:

Criteria for achievement level (performance standards)

Desirable characteristics for action (delivery standards)

Necessary core of knowledge (content standards)

Discussion about national standards consistently stresses that the standards are for all students. Yet, the National Council of Teachers of Mathematics produced a set of math standards, for example, that did not indicate how they would apply to students with disabilities. Experts in mathematics say that the proposed standards are appropriate but not feasible for students with disabilities.

Major standard-setting efforts now exist in most content areas: math, science, geography, history, civics, English, and arts. Groups have been formed in the areas of health and physical education and foreign language learning.

The Argument for High National Standards

The following paragraphs, excerpted from a report by the National Council on Educational Standards and Testing, present the case for establishing high national standards for all students. As you read, ask yourself what the proposed national standards mean for the inclusion process. Can the standards advocated apply to students with disabilities? If not, how do we ensure that students with disabilities are included in educational reform?

(Continued)

(Continued)

In the absence of well-defined and demanding standards, education in the United States has gravitated toward de facto national minimum expectations. Except for students who are planning to attend selective four-year colleges, current education standards focus on low-level reading and arithmetic skills and on small amounts of factual material in other content areas. Consumers of education in this country have settled for far less than they should and for far less than do their counterparts in other developed nations.

High national standards tied to assessments can create high expectations for all students and help to better target resources. They are critical to the nation in three primary ways: to promote educational equity, to preserve democracy and enhance the civic culture, and to improve economic competitiveness. Further, national education standards would help to provide an increasingly diverse and mobile population with shared values and knowledge. . . .

Providing genuine opportunity for all students to achieve high standards is a national moral imperative. The standards that the Council proposes would apply to the entire education system. All students must have the opportunity to achieve them and to be assessed fairly on their attainment. To bring this about, equitable educational opportunities must be provided. High quality standards and assessments should mobilize educators and the public to reform schools, engage families and communities, create incentives for high performance, and provide genuine opportunity for all students.

Source: National Council on Educational Standards and Testing (1992), pp. 2–3, 40.

Can standards be established that are both challenging for students who are gifted and inclusive of students with unique learning needs? Different standards may need to be set for students with disabilities. If so, how do we avoid creating separate educational systems for students with and without disabilities? Does setting standards perpetuate the tendency to exclude students with disabilities from state and national assessments? How should standards be set, and who should set them?

OPPORTUNITY-TO-LEARN STANDARDS

An important part of Goals 2000 was its encouragement for states to establish **opportunity-to-learn (OTL)** standards: the teaching and learning conditions necessary for all students to have a fair opportunity to learn, including ways of measuring the extent to which such standards are met. The OTL standards were to be developed by a task force and approved by NESIC. Over time, alternative definitions of OTL were debated, with no consensus. Defining OTL as time spent in school has implications for students with disabilities who attend school for partial days. Defining it in terms of resources allocated to instruction suggests that students with disabilities get more opportunity to learn because their education costs more. Defining OTL as time actively engaged in instruction implies inequities in measuring engaged time, especially for students who spend limited time actively responding to instruction.

A basic question about OTL, with regard to students with disabilities, is "Should students who are low functioning get

(a) the same amount of time as everybody else, or

(b) the amount of time necessary for them to be successful?"

Ysseldyke, Thurlow, and Shin (1994) prepared an extensive analysis of the concept of opportunity-to-learn and its potential impact on students with disabilities. The debate about OTL subsided early in the twenty-first century, and we hear little about it now.

SCHOOL RESTRUCTURING

School restructuring is a specific approach to school reform. It is "a systematic approach that acknowledges the complexity of fundamentally changing the way schools are organized in order to significantly increase student learning. It shifts the focus of reform from mandating what educators do to looking at the results their actions produce" (National Governors' Association, 1990, p. 1). In restructuring, efforts are made to reorganize schools to produce better results for students. Major reforms currently are underway in general education. They are proceeding on a piecemeal basis, with more talk than action about reform. Examples of restructuring include **site-based management** (decision making at the school site rather than a central office), changing staff roles, implementation of a higher-order-thinking curriculum (emphasis on strategies for learning, for example, rather than on basic skills), and adoption of an accountability system. Excellence—successful preparation of students for adulthood—is the desired outcome of reform and restructuring.

Kentucky School System Reform

Not all states have initiated such structural reform; some have been forced to change. In 1989, for example, the Kentucky State Supreme Court declared the entire state education system to be unconstitutional. Superintendents, local school boards, the state department of education, and, essentially, all educators were identified as part of the problem. The court ordered the revision of every aspect of the school system. Kentucky's response was to form a special task force and several working committees to make recommendations. Legislators put together a school-reform bill that has been called a "roadmap to reform" and "one of the most comprehensive restructuring efforts ever undertaken by a legislature" (Walker, 1990, p. 34–35). Features of the Kentucky reform, which was signed into law in April 1990, include

A system of rewards and sanctions for schools based on performance. Successful schools receive monetary rewards in the form of increased state subsidies. Unsuccessful schools are publicly identified and helped. Parents may use "choice" enrollment options to move their children out of unsatisfactory schools.

Outcomes-based focus. New techniques will be used to assess student achievement. Schools will be assessed on student health, dropout and retention rates, and attendance, as well as on student achievement.

Site-based management. Each district will have at least one site-based management school immediately, with all other schools phasing in by 1996.

IMPACT OF REFORM ON SPECIAL EDUCATION

When such radical reform takes place, the effects on special education and on those involved in it can be substantial. Teachers who participate in site-based management programs may find themselves helping to make basic policy decisions about special education: How should the school's available resources for special education be allocated? How many resource rooms should there be, and where? Who should teach? How should special education students be assessed? Are special education students eligible for supplemental education services from the same providers as those who serve general education students? In such a climate, teachers must be flexible and prepared to adapt to new conditions. For example, changing staff roles may require that special education teachers serve students after school rather than pulling students out of general education classes, or a new accountability system may require teachers to prove progress in more rigorous ways than they have used previously.

In some cases, too, restructuring may mean the establishment of a **unified system**, in which the distinctions between general education and special education are essentially abolished. Under such a plan, all students are merged into general education classes, and all educational funds are pooled. This kind of change can have profound effects on teachers who have students with special needs in their classrooms. In districts that engage in such radical restructuring, heavy demands may be put on teachers' resourcefulness and creativity. Concomitantly, though, teachers should have greater opportunities to contribute to fundamental improvements in their students' education.

3

Public Policy and School Reform in Perspective

S ocial, political, and economic factors change what happens in special education through their influence on current practice and on one another. When society's attitudes change toward the education of students who are exceptional, laws may be written or revised, and funding patterns may change. When funding patterns change, social attitudes may change, and so on. The relationships among factors that influence special education are evident in the impact of the Individuals With Disabilities Education Act (IDEA) (1997). IDEA has led to many changes in educational practice, the effects of which probably won't be known for years. Most educators contend that students with disabilities are receiving a more appropriate education now than they were in the early 1980s. Yet, because systematic collection of data on the outcomes of schooling for students with special needs only began in 2001, we can't prove it. States now are required to report annually on the performance and progress of all students, including students with disabilities. Over the next five years or so, we will have better data on the extent to which students with disabilities are meeting state standards. And, under both the No Child Left Behind Act (NCLB) and the Individuals With Disabilities Education Act (IDEA), schools can now be identified as "in need of improvement" when they are failing to meet standards for students with disabilities. The contention is that this will lead to interventions that will produce enhanced outcomes for students with disabilities. Again, only time will tell whether this actually happens.

Technology Helps a Teacher Meet New Roles and Stay Current

Kim Bazan, a classroom teacher, likes to keep up with new trends in education. She has read about education reform and the growing national concern for improving student outcomes. Moreover, some of the reform initiatives, including the movement toward greater inclusion, have taken hold in her school district. Ms. Bazan is not sure where she stands on inclusion. On the one hand, she believes that all students should have the opportunity to be successful and that teachers should be able to teach anyone who comes through the classroom door. On the other hand, she knows that students with disabilities learn best when classroom opportunities are structured to support their learning needs, and that not all teachers are prepared to make such changes. Because she is assuming new roles as a result of public policy changes influencing special education, Ms. Bazan believes that staying current is more pressing than ever.

To find out more about perspectives on inclusion, Ms. Bazan enrolled in an interactive TV course offered by her state department of education and the community college in her area. She attended class at a local high school with several other teachers. The course was taught by a professor in another city. About 70 teachers at 15 sites participated, using TV monitors with split-screen technology and carefully designed course segments. Ms. Bazan used her home computer to download assignments and send responses to the professor. She also used her computer to communicate with other students in the class.

Ms. Bazan also uses her home computer and the Internet to keep in touch with colleagues across the country.

In this way, she receives up-to-date information on tactics for helping her students with disabilities remain in classes with their nondisabled neighbors and peers. From time to time, she downloads information from electronic bulletin boards and shares it with her colleagues at school. When she needs information, Ms. Bazan posts a message using e-mail or connects to her local library and searches the card catalog for new books. She has also attended inservice workshops on strategies and tactics for effective instruction and simple ways to make teaching fun.

There is no question that special education is changing and that public policy changes are influencing teachers. Ms. Bazan knows that keeping up means taking advantage of innovations in technology and teacher preparation methods. By working with students with disabilities on a daily basis, she has come to appreciate technology not as a magic potion but as a useful and important resource.

IMPACT OF LAWS ON
SPECIAL EDUCATION

For decades, special education existed as a system parallel to general education. With the enactment of the Education for All Handicapped Children Act (1975) and the requirement that students with disabilities be educated in the **least restrictive environment** (that is, in general education environments or in environments that are as much like general education as possible), special education became part of a continuum of delivering services to students. The Education for All Handicapped Children Act forged a new partnership between special and general education. For the first time, schools were challenged with educating new populations of students with severe disabilities, both younger (ages 3 to 5) and older (ages 18 to 21). With the passage of the Individuals With Disabilities Education Act (IDEA) in 1990 and its amendments in 1997, school personnel were confronted with educating students with disabilities from birth to 21 and with developing transition plans that enable students to enter the world of work. IDEA also required schools to enter cooperative arrangements with other agencies to provide related services and to pay for those services. An era of interagency collaboration and cooperation was born.

CURRENT REFORMS

With school reform, school restructuring, the establishment of national education goals, passage of the NCLB, and the push for full inclusion, special education is continuing to change. Some districts are merging all types of education—general, compensatory, and special—into a single system. In other districts, the ultimate impact of the reform movements is not yet known. The transformations raise fundamental questions about the long-term effects on the education of students who are exceptional. The Individuals With Disabilities Education Act was revised and reauthorized in 2004.

IMPORTANCE OF TEACHER TRAINING

One area that has felt the impact of change is teacher training. To provide services to new populations of students with medical or physical disabilities, schools need specially trained teachers—teachers who can run portable respirators, use augmentative devices to communicate with nonoral children, clean wounds, and bandage children with spina bifida. General education teachers, charged with the task of educating students with disabilities in their classrooms, need inservice training. If schools do not have the financial resources to give them that training, teachers are faced with the task of providing services they are not trained to do, and they develop job-related stress. Many teachers then change jobs; others leave the profession altogether.

THE FUTURE OF SPECIAL EDUCATION

There are various ways to meet the special learning needs of students. Are services being provided in the best possible way? As Biklen (1989) put it, "states could fund the education of all students without identifying any students or programs as special, but they do not. Persistence in funding labeled students or programs may reflect concern that students with disabilities would not receive much-needed special services if unlabeled" (p. 9). Special education could be freed from the "stepchild" role it sometimes is forced to play. Its future could be different, if people learning about special education are encouraged to think differently about it. In 1983, Mary Moran wrote, "alternative futures can be imagined, if we free ourselves to question assumptions" (p. 36).

Important decisions have to be made about the future of special education; many will be made by the students of today who will teach the students of tomorrow. This is your challenge, your social responsibility.

CLOSING COMMENTS AND PARTING THOUGHTS

Two fundamental assumptions are driving the development of U.S. educational policy, and the way these assumptions are played out in practice will affect what happens to students who are exceptional. First, Americans assume we can have both excellence and equity in the education of students. This assumption has two premises. The first premise is that for our democracy and our economy to remain strong, we need a well-skilled workforce. The kinds of skills needed to survive in our increasingly complex world are changing, but students still must have high-level skills. The second premise is that *all* students, including those with disabilities, must have the opportunity to learn to the same high-content standards. All students are capable of learning more than they now learn, and they have the capability of learning complex content. No one should be left out. At the same time, however, we don't always know precisely what to do with each student.

The second fundamental assumption is that schools cannot operate in isolation to get students to achieve standards. This means that teachers, nurses, occupational therapists, psychologists, counselors, and social workers have to form alliances with other professionals to meet students' needs. The challenges students bring to schools are increasingly complex, and no one discipline can meet their needs in isolation. Interdisciplinary and multidisciplinary activities are required.

There are two ways to make major contributions to the instruction of students who are exceptional. First, lead in the appropriate instruction of these students. Strong leadership is needed to achieve broad moral obligations. Second, apply basic principles of effective instruction, such as those discussed throughout the books that comprise this series, *A Practical Approach to Special Education for Every Teacher*.

There is no magic trick to make your teaching life better. We hope this module helps you to become a better teacher. But prescriptions and advice have only limited value; teaching is hard work. The future is yours. We leave you with ten tips to use as you make the journey we call teaching:

1. Always deliver more than you promise.

2. Keep records of methods that work.

3. Be cheerful and enthusiastic, even when you don't feel like it.

4. Dream big dreams, but be known for what you do.

5. Don't be afraid to make mistakes, but be sure to learn from them.

6. Encourage every student to be an expert at something.

7. Teach by this adage: You don't have to be sick to get better.

8. Avoid paralysis by analysis.

9. Teach students to tell the principal how much they enjoy being in your class.

10. Never eat anything in the lunchroom covered completely with brown gravy.

4

What Have We Learned?

As you complete your study of public policy, school reform and special education, it may be helpful to review what you have learned. To help you check your understanding, we have listed the key points and key vocabulary for you to review. We have included the Self-Assessment again, so you can compare what you know now with what you knew as you began your study. Finally, we provide a few topics for you to think about and some activities for you to do "on your own."

KEY POINTS

▣ Special education is driven more by social, political, and economic factors than by actual changes in education.

▣ People's values, opinions, and beliefs influence how limited resources are distributed.

▣ The general political climate (conservative versus liberal), the political actions of families and advocacy groups, and the work of legislatures and the courts have a significant influence on special education policy and practice.

◩ Services to students with disabilities are funded differently in different states, which influences who gets services and the nature of interventions.

◩ Some of the most far-reaching school-reform efforts involve school restructuring, an approach that stresses the need for fundamental change in the way schools are organized.

◩ Two fundamental assumptions underlie the development of current legislation on goals, standards, and assessments: (1) We can have both excellence and equity in education, and (2) Schools cannot operate in isolation to get students to achieve standards.

KEY VOCABULARY

Advocacy groups are groups intending either to encourage or prevent specific public policy changes by influencing policy makers.

Allocation of funds is the process by which state legislatures distribute both state and federal moneys to local education agencies.

Categorical programs specialize in treating students with specific kinds of disabilities (e.g., blindness, communication disorders).

Classification refers to the practice of grouping like individuals or items together. In special education, it means the process of deciding that some students are mentally retarded, others gifted, and still others learning disabled, etc.

Early intervention refers to services provided to young children (and their families) who have special needs that could influence development.

Inclusion means including students with special needs in general education programs to the extent that these students can be successful.

Larry P v Riles is a legal decision forbidding the state of California from using intelligence tests to place African American students in classes for students with mental retardation.

Least Restrictive Envirnoment means that, to the maximum extent appropriate, children with disabilities are to be educated with children who are not disabled, and special classes, separate schooling, or other removal of children with disabilities from the regular educational envirnoment occurs only when the nature or severity of the disability of a child is such that education in regular classes with the use of supplementary aids and services cannot be achieved satisfactorily.

National Education Goals were originally stated in 1984 and again in 1994, and were intended to improve education by defining specific objectives for students, educators, and parents.

No Child Left Behind Act was authorized in 2001 and mandates state accountability for student outcomes by requiring evidence of student progress.

Office of Special Education Programs (OSEP) is a division of the U.S. Department of Education that oversees funding issues related to special education.

Opportunity-to-learn standards are the teaching and learning conditions necessary for all students to have a fair opportunity to learn, including ways of measuring the extent to which such standards are met.

Regular education initiative is a proposal aimed at increasing the shared responsibility of both special educators and general educators for the education of students with disabilities.

Related services are the supportive services required to assist a child with a disability to benefit from special education (e.g., physical therapy, transportation, speech and language pathology services).

School restructuring means reorganizing schools in an effort to obtain better results for students. An example: grouping 3rd, 4th, and 5th graders together for instruction and doing the same with 6th, 7th, and 8th graders.

Site-based management is a method of restructuring where decision making occurs at the school site rather than at a central office.

Standards are statements of criteria in education against which comparisons can be made.

Unified system is a method of restructuring where the distinctions between general education and special education are essentially abolished.

U.S. Office of Civil Rights strives to ensure equal access to education and advocates for those who may be discriminated against.

Self-Assessment 2

A fter you complete this book, check your knowledge and understanding of the content covered. Choose the best answer for each of the following questions:

1. Which of the following is NOT a driving force behind change in special education?

   a. Social factors

   b. Political factors

   c. Personal factors

   d. Economic factors

2. In recent years, while the number of students classified as having mental retardation has decreased, those classified as having learning disabilities has _____.

   a. Decreased

   b. Increased

   c. Stayed the same

   d. Doubled

3. Head Start is an example of a(n) _____, a way to help disadvantaged children acquire learning readiness skills.

   a. Early intervention

   b. Special education

   c. Site-based management

   d. Advocacy group

4. Which of the following currently provides the most funding for public education?

a. Local governments

b. State governments

c. Federal government

d. Private foundations

5. No Child Left Behind mandates which of the following?

a. Content standards

b. Lifelong learning

c. Spending

d. Accountability

6. Which of the following was NOT addressed in "Goals 2000," an education plan created in 1994 by George H. W. Bush and endorsed by Bill Clinton?

a. Mathematics and science

b. Parental participation

c. Students with special needs

d. Teacher education and professional development

7. Site-based management includes which of the following restructuring changes?

a. Decision making at the central office

b. Changing staff roles

c. Emphasis on basic skills

d. Budget cuts

8. Which of the following is NOT an example of a standard?

a. Criteria for achievement level

b. Desirable characteristic for action

c. Necessary core of knowledge

d. Important piece of information

9. A system which abolishes the distinctions between general education and special education is known as a _____.

a. Unified system

b. Partial system

c. Conglomerate system

d. Modern system

10. For a given student, the "least restrictive environment" could be a _____.

a. General education classroom

b. Special education classroom

c. General education classroom with support

d. All of the above

REFLECTION

- Identify three alternative explanations for why special education services may be different in Detroit, Miami, and Missoula, Montana.
- What are three major things that happened to public education as a result of passage of the No Child Left Behind Act?
- In this chapter, we argue that education in the U.S. is driven by two goals: excellence and equity. Describe these twin goals, and indicate briefly how schools might possibly work to meet both.

Answer Key for Self-Assessments

1. c

2. b

3. a

4. b

5. d

6. c

7. b

8. d

9. a

10. d

On Your Own

☑ Develop a list of actions you believe could be taken by elementary or secondary schools to lower the U.S. dropout rate. Then get together with a small group of classmates and compare your lists. Create one comprehensive list and reach agreement on the three actions you believe are the most important. Share and compare your group's list with your entire class.

☑ Identify the way funding decisions are made in your state, and obtain a list of the percentages of students served in each disability category. Then obtain the percentages from two other states whose funding formulas differ. Discuss the extent to which the number of students served is a function of the ways funding decisions are made. Read *Civic Report 32: Effects of Funding Incentives on Special Education Enrollment* (Greene & Forster, 2002).

☑ Find out the major educational goals of your state department of education and the activities of your state to meet those goals. How consistent are your state's goals with those listed in Goals 2000?

Resources

BOOKS

Lane, J. L., & Epps, E. (1992). *Restructuring schools.* Berkeley, CA: McCutchan. This book provides national and international case studies and an analysis of the challenges involved in restructuring schools.

McLaughlin, M. J., & Warren, S. H. (1992). *Issues and options in restructuring schools and special education programs.* College Park, MD: University of Maryland Policy Options Center. This book explores the issues affecting the delivery of educational services to students with disabilities within the context of educational restructuring.

Sizer, T. (1992). *Horace's school. Redesigning the American high school.* Boston: Houghton Mifflin. This plan for secondary-school reform is proposed by a leading expert in the field of education.

Ysseldyke, J. E., Algozzine, B. A., & Thurlow, M. L. (2000). *Critical issues in special education* (5th ed.). Boston: Houghton Mifflin. This text provides a critical analysis of major social, political, and economic issues in special education.

JOURNALS AND ARTICLES

Disability Studies Quarterly. This journal is published online by the Center on Disability Studies. *www.cds.hawaii.edu/dsq.*

Education Policy Analysis Archives. This online archive has many full text articles on policy and education. *http://olam.ed.asu .edu/epaa/.*

Journal of Disability Policy Studies. This journal publishes discussion, reviews, and research on a wide range of disability policy topics. Department of Rehabilitation and Research, University of Arkansas, 346 N. West Ave., Fayetteville, AK 72701. *www.uark.edu/~kens/dispol/JDPS/.*

Society for Disability Studies. This society provides an online portal with links to many areas of disability research and policy issues. *www.uic.edu/orgs/sds/links.html.*

ORGANIZATIONS

American Federation of Teachers (AFT)

AFT is a union that strongly supports special education, advocating for appropriate teacher and paraprofessional training and proper inclusion practices. AFT, AFL-CIO, 555 New Jersey Ave. N.W., Washington, DC 20001. www.aft.org.

Council for Exceptional Children (CEC)

The CEC advocates for educational improvements for people with disabilities and helps professionals obtain the resources and conditions needed for effective practice. CEC, 1100 North Glebe Road, Suite 300,Arlington, VA 22201–5704. (703) 620-3660. (888) CEC-SPED. TTY: (703) 264-9446. www.cec .sped.org.

Learning Disabilities Association of America (LDA).

LDA is a nonprofit organization of 40,000 members that advances the education of people with disabilities. LDA, 4156 Liberty Road, Pittsburgh, PA 15234–1349. (412) 341-1515.www .ldanatl.org.

References

Biklen, D. (1989). Redefining education. In D. Biklen, D. Ferguson, & A. Ford (Eds.), *Schooling and disability* (pp. 1–24). Chicago: National Society for the Study of Education.

Education for All Handicapped Children Act, Pub. L. No. 94-142, 89 Stat. 773 (1975).

Goals 2000: The Educate America Act, Pub. L. No. 103-227, 108 Stat. 125 (1994).

Greene, J. P., & Forster, G. (2002). *Civic report 32: Effects of funding incentives on special education enrollment.* New York: Manhattan Institute.

Individuals With Disabilities Education Act, Pub. L. No. 101-476, 104 Stat. 1141 (1990).

Individuals With Disabilities Education Act, Pub. L. No. 105-17, 111 Stat. 37 (1997).

Individuals With Disabilities Education Act, Pub. L. No. 108-444, 118 Stat. 2647 (2004).

Larry P. v. Riles, 343 F. Supp. 1306 (N.D. Cal. 1972) aff'd, 502 F.2d 963 (9th Cir. 1974).

Moran, M. (1983). Inventing a future for special education: A cautionary tale. *Journal for Special Educators, 19,* 28–36.

National Commission on Excellence in Education. (1983). *A nation at risk: The imperative for educational reform.* Washington, DC: Author.

National Council on Educational Standards and Testing. (1992). *Raising standards for American education: A report to Congress, the Secretary of Education, the National Education Goals Panel, and the American people.* Washington, DC: Author.

National Governors' Association. (1989). *Time for results.* Washington, DC: Author.

National Governors' Association. (1990). *State actions to restructure schools: First steps.* Washington, DC: Author.

No Child Left Behind Act, Pub. L. No. 107-110, 115 Stat. 1425 (2001).

Reading Excellence Act, Pub. L. No. 105-277, 112 Stat. 2681–2756 (1998).

Stern, J. (1988). *The condition of education: Elementary and secondary education.* Washington, DC: National Center for Education Statistics.

Thurlow, M. L., Wiley, H. I., & Bielinski, J. (2002). *Biennial performance reports: 2000–2001 state assessment data.* Minneapolis, MN: National Center on Educational Outcomes.

U.S. Department of Education. (2001). To assure the free and appropriate public education of all children with disabilities. *Twenty-third annual report to Congress on the implementation of the Individuals With Disabilities Education Act.* Washington, DC: Author.

Walker, R. (1990, April 11). Lawmakers in Kentucky approve landmark school-reform bill. *Education Week, 10*(1), 34–35.

White House. (1990). *National goals for education* [Press release]. Washington, DC: Author.

Ysseldyke, J. E., Algozzine, B., & Thurlow, M. L. (2000). *Critical issues in special education.* Boston: Houghton Mifflin.

Ysseldyke, J. E., Thurlow, M. L., & Shin, H. (1994). *Opportunity to learn and students with disabilities* (Synthesis Report 14). Minneapolis, MN: University of Minnesota National Center on Educational Outcomes.

Index

Note: Numbers in **Bold** followed by a colon [:] denote the book number within which the page numbers are found.

**CORWIN
PRESS**

The Corwin Press logo—a raven striding across an open book— represents the union of courage and learning. Corwin Press is committed to improving education for all learners by publishing books and other professional development resources for those serving the field of PreK–12 education. By providing practical, hands-on materials, Corwin Press continues to carry out the promise of its motto: **"Helping Educators Do Their Work Better."**